Second baseman Bobby Lowe

THE STORY OF THE ATLANTA BRAVES

First baseman Matt Olson

THE STORY OF THE

ATLANTA BRAVES

MICHAEL E. GOODMAN

Third baseman Chipper Jones

CREATIVE EDUCATION / CREATIVE PAPERBACKS

Published by Creative Education and Creative Paperbacks
P.O. Box 227, Mankato, Minnesota 56002
Creative Education and Creative Paperbacks are imprints of
The Creative Company
www.thecreativecompany.us

Book Design by Wyeth Morgan
Art direction by Blue Design (www.bluedes.com)

Images by Alamy Stock Photo/Cal Sport Media, 29; Associated Press/Gerald Herbert, cover; Getty Images/CHRIS WILKINS, 7 (bottom, left), Edward M. Pio Roda, 22–23, Eliot J. Schechter, 7 (top, right), HENNY RAY ABRAMS, 6 (top, right), John Adams/Icon Sportswire, 19, Louis Requena/MLB, cover, 18, Mary DeCicco, 2, MATT CAMPBELL, 3, Mike Zarrilli, 26–27, MONICA M. DAVEY, 4–5, 6 (top, left), 32, National Baseball Hall of Fame Library, 12, Otto Greule Jr, 9, Photo File, 20, Rick Stewart, 25, Robert Riger, 15, 16, Ron Vesely, 6 (bottom, left), Ronald C. Modra, 7 (bottom, right), Scott Cunningham, 6 (bottom, right), 7 (top, left), Todd Kirkland, 30, 31; Library of Congress/Howe, F. L., 11; public domain/10; Wikimedia Commons/Mort Rogers scorecard, 10, public domain, 1

Every effort has been made to contact copyright holders for material reproduced in this book. Any omissions will be rectified in subsequent printings if notice is given to the publisher.

Library of Congress Cataloging-in-Publication Data
Names: Goodman, Michael E. author
Title: The story of the Atlanta Braves / Michael E. Goodman.
Description: Mankato, Minnesota : Creative Education and Creative Paperbacks, 2026. | Series: Creative sports. Major League Baseball | Includes index. | Audience: Ages 8-12 | Audience: Grades 4-6 | Summary: "Discover the Atlanta Braves' thrilling journey across three cities, featuring legendary players and the Major League Baseball team's most iconic moments. Written for middle-grade readers. Includes table of contents, sidebars, and index"– Provided by publisher.
Identifiers: LCCN 2025013179 (print) | LCCN 2025013180 (ebook) | ISBN 9798895810859 library binding | ISBN 9798896800385 paperback | ISBN 9798895812112 ebook
Subjects: LCSH: Atlanta Braves (Baseball team)–History–Juvenile literature
Classification: LCC GV875.A8 G667 2026 (print) | LCC GV875.A8 (ebook) | DDC 796.357/6409758231–dc23
LC record available at https://lccn.loc.gov/2025013179
LC ebook record available at https://lccn.loc.gov/2025013180

Printed in the United States

Pitcher Greg Maddux

Atlanta

3
Braves

3

Braves

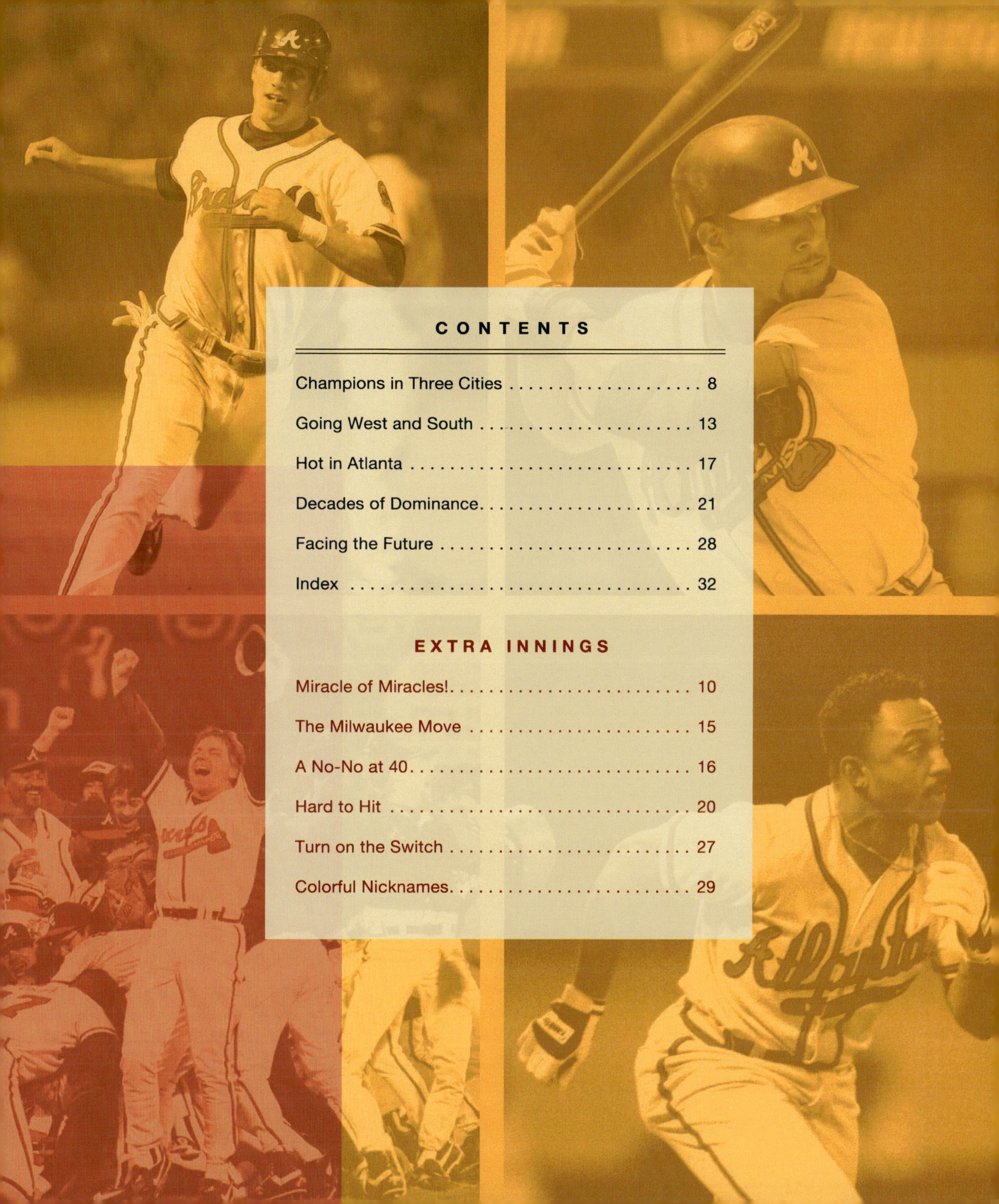

CONTENTS

EXTRA INNINGS

CHAMPIONS IN THREE CITIES

Atlanta-Fulton County Stadium was rocking on October 25, 1995. The hometown Atlanta Braves were locked in a tense 0–0 battle with the Cleveland Indians in Game 6 of the World Series. Atlanta was up three games to two in the series. One more win would give the Braves franchise its first championship since moving to Atlanta in 1966. Braves star lefty Tom Glavine had blanked the Indians on only one hit through the first five innings of Game 6. But Atlanta still hadn't broken through on Cleveland lefty Jim Poole either.

Before the Braves came to bat in the bottom of the sixth inning, Glavine confidently told his teammates, "Come on, boys, get me one (run) because they're not getting any." Slugging outfielder David Justice got Glavine's message and promptly led off the sixth with a home run into the right-field stands. That was enough. Three innings later, the game ended with the score still 1–0, and the Braves were world champions for the third time in their history.

The Braves' first two World Series triumphs had come years earlier while playing in two different cities far from Atlanta—Boston, Massachusetts, and Milwaukee, Wisconsin.

Outfielder David Justice

EXTRA INNINGS

MIRACLE OF MIRACLES!

Why was the 1914 Braves' season such a miracle? Between 1904 and 1913, the club had averaged 100 losses each year. Then, in 1914, its record was 94–59. Star pitcher Bill James won 26 games in 1914 and two games in the World Series. In his career, he won only six games before 1914 and only five games after that season. In still another miracle, the rival Boston Red Sox allowed the Braves to play their World Series home games at Fenway Park. It was newer and larger than rickety South End Grounds, their usual home field. Even the Red Sox seemed proud of the Braves that year!

Boston Beaneaters, 1886

The club was founded in 1871 as the Boston Red Stockings. It was part of a new professional league called the National Association (NA). The Red Stockings dominated the NA for five years, winning four league titles. Their record in 1875 was an amazing 71 wins and 8 losses—an .899 winning percentage! The next year, Boston moved to the newly formed National League (NL), and the franchise has been a part of the NL ever since. Over the next 36 years, the club competed under such names as the Beaneaters, Doves, and Rustlers. It officially became the Boston Braves in 1912. The team owner had chosen the name because he belonged to a political group that called its members "Braves."

Those early Boston teams continued to win a lot of games. By 1898, they had captured eight NL pennants. The team's star hitter was 5-foot-7 outfielder Hugh Duffy. He set an all-time major league record in 1894 when he batted .440. (That year, he also led the NL in home runs with 18.) The club's top pitcher was Charles "Kid" Nichols, who won 30 or more games seven times in the 1890s. His 362 career wins still rank seventh in major league history.

Boston fell on hard times in the early 1900s, however. When veteran manager George Stallings took over in 1913, he faced a group of players who were poorly paid and poorly prepared. He put the club through endless drills. The hard work began to pay off midway through the 1914 season. The Braves were mired in last

place on July 4. Then something remarkable happened. Boston won 61 of its last 81 games and captured the NL pennant. The Braves then stormed into the World Series against the heavily favored Philadelphia Athletics. Behind the outstanding pitching of Dick Rudolph and Bill James, Boston swept the series in four games. Baseball writers called them the "Miracle Braves."

Sadly, there were no more miracles after that. The team sank back near the bottom of the NL and stayed there until the mid-1940s. Finally, in 1946, two young pitchers—righty Johnny Sain and lefty Warren Spahn—arrived in Boston and buoyed the hopes of Braves fans. They led the club on an amazing stretch in 1948 to capture the club's first NL pennant in 34 years. Then each posted one victory in the World Series. But the Braves still came up short, falling to the Cleveland Indians, four games to two. It would be nine years before the Braves returned to the World Series. By then, they would be based more than 1,000 miles to the west in Milwaukee, Wisconsin.

GOING WEST AND SOUTH

Losing the 1948 World Series took a toll on the Boston Braves—and their fans. The club struggled both to win games and to sell tickets. Luckily, two outstanding players arrived in the early 1950s. Speedy center fielder Sam Jethroe, a veteran of the Negro Leagues, was the first African American to play for the Braves. He earned NL Rookie of the Year honors in 1950 at age 33. Two years later, rookie infielder Eddie Mathews started off his Hall of Fame career by smashing 25 homers.

Mathews continued to star in 1953. But his Braves hat now featured an "M" instead of a "B." Owner Lou Perini had moved the team from

1914 World Series, Boston Braves vs. Philadelphia Athletics

Boston to Milwaukee at the start of the 1953 season. The Braves showed immediate improvement on the field. They finished 92–62 in their first year in Milwaukee. A league-high 1.8 million hometown fans packed County Stadium to cheer on the club. Mathews led the major leagues with 47 home runs. Spahn topped the NL with 23 victories. Young pitcher Lew Burdette added 15 wins, thanks to his amazing fast-dropping sinkerball.

Milwaukee fans cheered even louder when rookie Hank Aaron arrived in 1954. Aaron took over in right field and stayed there for the next 20 years. At 6 feet tall and just 180 pounds, Aaron did not look like a typical slugger. But he generated power with his strong wrists. "I turn my wrists over," he explained. "My right hand turns over toward the pitcher, so when I hit the ball there's a rotation on it that makes the ball go a long way." His powerful drives soon earned him the nickname "Hammerin' Hank." Aaron set new major-league standards for career home runs, runs batted in (RBI), extra-base hits, and total bases. Some of his records still stand today.

The Braves built a powerhouse in Milwaukee. Mathews, Aaron, and first baseman Joe Adcock took charge in the field. Spahn, Burdette, and Bob Buhl led from the mound. Working together, the Braves edged out the St. Louis Cardinals for the 1957 NL pennant. Then they faced off against the defending champion New York Yankees in the World Series. Burdette's sinker proved unbeatable. He defeated the Yankees 4–2 in Game 2 and then pitched shutouts in Games 5 and 7. Burdette was not supposed to pitch in Game 7. But when Spahn came down with the flu, Burdette stepped in. He threw a masterpiece on two days' rest, leading the Braves to their second world championship.

The same clubs met again in the 1958 World Series. This time, New York came out on top. Afterward, the Braves started to fade again. Fans began staying away from the ballpark. Management decided another move was in

EXTRA INNINGS

THE MILWAUKEE MOVE

When the Braves moved to Milwaukee in 1953, they were the first major league franchise to relocate in 50 years. The move went smoothly for several reasons. First, many Milwaukee fans were already Braves fans. The city's minor league club, the Brewers, was a top farm team for the Braves. Several Milwaukee minor league stars, such as shortstop Johnny Logan and pitcher Dick Donovan, had moved on to Boston as major leaguers. Second, Milwaukee already had a stadium with seating for more than 36,000 fans and parking for more than 10,000 cars. Third, a close friend of the Braves' owner ran a big local brewery and promised to buy lots of advertising.

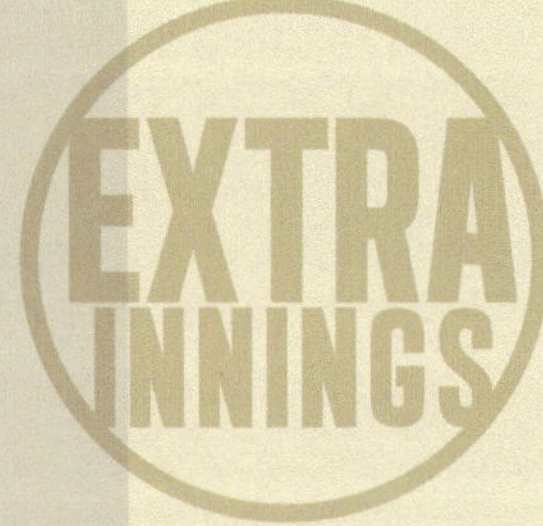

WARREN SPAHN
PITCHER
BRAVES SEASONS: 1942, 1946–64
6-FOOT-0, 172 POUNDS
INDUCTED INTO THE HALL OF FAME IN 1974
NAMED TO 17 NL ALL-STAR TEAMS
WON 363 GAMES (MOST EVER BY A LEFTY)
LED NL IN WINS EIGHT TIMES

A NO-NO AT 40

On April 28, 1961, five days after his 40th birthday, Warren Spahn tossed a no-hitter against the San Francisco Giants. The Braves (then in Milwaukee) scored one run on a first-inning Hank Aaron single, and that was enough for Spahn to win the 1–0 thriller. Only two Giants reached base, both on walks. Amazingly, Spahn had also pitched a no-hitter the year before, when he was 39. "This is ridiculous. A fellow my age shouldn't be pitching no-hitters," Spahn said after the game. "Here I pitch 15 years in the National League and don't get a no-hitter. Then, bingo, I've got two. How do you figure it?"

order. This time, the team headed south. It hoped to build a new fan base in fast-growing Atlanta, Georgia.

HOT IN ATLANTA

Before the Braves arrived in Atlanta in 1966, southeastern baseball fans had never had their own major league team. They quickly fell in love with the club. Meanwhile, Braves hitters fell in love with offense-friendly Atlanta–Fulton County Stadium. Aaron led the league with 44 home runs in 1966. Catcher Joe Torre and first baseman/outfielder Felipe Alou each smacked more than 30 homers. All three were named to the All-Star team that year.

In 1969, the Braves soared to the top of the NL West Division. They faced the surprising New York Mets in the NL Championship Series (NLCS). The excitement in Atlanta faded when the Mets swept the Braves in three games. After the disappointing loss, the team fell into a tailspin. It did not earn another postseason berth for 13 years.

In the meantime, Braves fans still had lots to cheer about. In 1973, Hammerin' Hank began a serious pursuit of Babe Ruth's career home run record of 714. Not everyone wanted Aaron, an African American, to break Ruth's mark. He received hate mail and threats as he neared the record. Then, several reporters wrote about the hate-mail barrage. Aaron began receiving thousands of letters of support. The 39-year-old slugger had a remarkable season. He smashed 40 homers, drove in 96 runs, and batted .301. But Aaron was still one home run shy of the record. He tied the Yankees' legend during his first at bat

Right fielder Hank Aaron

in 1974. Four days later, he blasted number 715 into the Braves' left field bullpen. Aaron finished his career in 1976 with 755 homers. That record lasted more than 30 years. Barry Bonds of the San Francisco Giants surpassed it in 2007.

While Aaron spearheaded the offense, knuckleball specialist Phil Niekro was the club's mound ace. Niekro's knuckler seemed to dance on its way toward the plate. It was tricky for batters to hit and difficult for Braves' catchers to glove. During his 21-year Braves career, the iron-armed Niekro won 268 games, third-most in franchise history behind Warren Spahn and Kid Nichols. Niekro eventually joined Spahn, Aaron, and Mathews in the Hall of Fame.

During the 1980s, Atlanta's top star was outfielder Dale Murphy. From 1982 through 1987, Murphy averaged 36 homers and 105 RBI per season. He won five Gold Glove awards for his superb fielding. He was named Most Valuable Player (MVP) in both 1982 and 1983. Murphy also received several awards for his humanitarian activities. "If the Hall of Fame is looking for stars who were role models, they couldn't find anybody better than Dale," Niekro noted.

Outfielder Ronald Acuña Jr.

PHIL NIEKRO
PITCHER
BRAVES SEASONS: 1964–83, 1987
6-FOOT-1, 180 POUNDS
INDUCTED INTO THE HALL OF FAME IN 1997
NAMED TO 5 NL ALL-STAR TEAMS
WON 300TH GAME AT AGE 46
PHIL AND JOE NIEKRO TOGETHER WON 539 GAMES (MOST EVER BY BROTHERS)

HARD TO HIT

When Phil Niekro began playing minor league baseball in the Braves system, he was a "normal" pitcher, throwing mostly fastballs and curves. But he wasn't standing out. He was reluctant to use a secret weapon his father had taught him, a slow-moving knuckleball that seemed to float toward the plate. One day, his minor league manager told him to "throw the knuckler or go home." The special pitch changed his career. Niekro's knuckleball tosses twisted batters into knots. "Trying to hit him is like trying to eat Jell-O with chopsticks," said opposing outfielder Bobby Murcer.

DECADES OF DOMINANCE

The Braves ended the 1990 season with the worst record in the major leagues (65–97). Then the team made an amazing turnaround in 1991, topping the NL West with 94 wins.. The Braves even came within one game of winning the 1991 World Series against the Minnesota Twins. The next season, the team made its second straight World Series appearance but lost again, this time to the Toronto Blue Jays. Still, something extraordinary was happening in Atlanta.

Throughout the 1990s and into the 2000s, the Braves won more games than any other NL team. They topped their division 14 times in 15 years. However, Atlanta won the World Series just once during that time. That championship came in 1995, with manager Bobby Cox at the helm. The 1995 Braves featured three of the league's best pitchers: Greg Maddux, Tom Glavine, and John Smoltz. All three would later be elected to the Hall of Fame. Maddux led the way in 1995, winning 19 games and losing only 2. He earned his fourth consecutive Cy Young Award as the league's best pitcher. A master of control, Maddux rarely walked a batter. The hitting leaders were third baseman Chipper Jones, outfielders David Justice and Ryan Klesko, and first baseman Fred McGriff. Each slugged more than 20 homers in 1995. Justice's deep rightfield blast in Game 6 of the World Series against the Indians broke a 0–0 tie and propelled the Braves to the crown. When Atlanta outfielder Marquis Grissom caught the last out in the ninth inning, TV announcer Bob Costas proclaimed, "The team of the '90s has its World Championship at last."

Shortstop Dansby Swanson

26

Atlanta continued adding talent as the new millennium began. Slugging right fielder Gary Sheffield and multitalented center fielder Andruw Jones added punch to the Braves' lineup. Jones displayed an amazing combination of speed and power. He had outstanding fielding instincts, too. During his time in Atlanta, he smacked 368 home runs and won 10 Gold Gloves. One of the first MLB players from the Caribbean island of Curacao, Jones quickly became a hero in his homeland.

In 2006, the Braves failed to reach the postseason for the first time in 16 years. This marked the start of a down period in Atlanta. The team teetered between winning and losing seasons for the next decade. But a few gems gleamed through the rough era.

In 2007, Chipper Jones became the first Braves player to record 2,000 hits. In July, he surpassed Dale Murphy for the third-most home runs in franchise history. The versatile third baseman/outfielder also began a dramatic run for the NL batting title. He lost out on the last day of the season to Colorado Rockies left fielder Matt Holliday. Jones would not be denied the following season. He batted over .400 in April and May before "slipping" into the .390s in late June. By season's end, his average stood at a league-best .364. "He almost won the batting title last year, and he won it this year," Cox said. "This is just one more notch into the Hall of Fame for him." Jones did indeed earn his spot in the Hall of Fame in 2018, six years after retiring as a Braves player.

1995 World Series, Game 4

CHIPPER JONES
THIRD BASE, OUTFIELD
BRAVES SEASONS: 1993–2012
6-FOOT-4, 210 POUNDS
INDUCTED INTO THE HALL OF FAME IN 2018
NAMED TO 8 NL ALL-STAR TEAMS
WON NL BATTING TITLE IN 2008 (.364)
HIGHEST LIFETIME BATTING AVERAGE BY A SWITCH-HITTER (.303)

EXTRA INNINGS

TURN ON THE SWITCH

When he started playing baseball at age six, Chipper Jones batted strictly right-handed. Then his father, a high school baseball coach, worked on improving his left-hand swing. He hoped to turn Chipper into a switch-hitter, like his idol, Yankees' great Mickey Mantle. It worked. Chipper became so effective hitting from both sides of the plate that he was the top overall pick in the 1990 Major League Baseball draft. And his switch-hitting prowess helped him earn his way to the Hall of Fame. Other switch-hitters usually have a "best" side, but not Chipper. During his 18-year career, he batted .303 as a righty and .304 as a lefty.

FACING THE FUTURE

Starting in 2010, the Braves went through a lot of turnover. Even Bobby Cox called it quits following that season. In 25 seasons as team manager, Cox amassed a club-record 2,149 wins.

Chipper Jones retired following the 2012 season. But new stars were on the horizon. First baseman Freddie Freeman—an outstanding batter and fielder—became a starter in 2011. He quickly established himself as an All-Star. Right fielder Nick Markakis arrived via trade before the 2015 season. He made an immediate impact on both offense and defense, winning both a Gold Glove and Silver Slugger award.

In 2017, second baseman Ozzie Albies joined shortstop Dansby Swanson at Atlanta's new Truist Park. Together, they became one of the youngest double-play combos in the league. Swanson had grown up just outside Atlanta, and local fans loved him right away. The 5-foot-8 Albies, a native of Curacao, had surprising power. He reminded some Atlanta fans of his fellow countryman and former Braves standout, Andruw Jones.

The pieces came together in late April 2018. A new shining star, Venezuelan outfielder Ronald Acuña Jr., made his major league debut. He batted .293 with 26 homers and was the runaway winner for NL Rookie of the Year. The team topped the NL East and returned to the playoffs for the first time in five seasons. They have continued to reach the playoffs each year through 2024.

After setting a franchise record with 249 home runs in 2019, the Braves were ready for a breakout season in 2020. Then the Covid-19 pandemic struck. The season didn't begin until late July and was shortened to only 60

Ronald Acuña Jr., also known as "La Bestia"

COLORFUL NICKNAMES

Many Braves players have had unusual nicknames. The 1914 "Miracle Braves" included Hall of Fame infielders Walter "Rabbit" Maranville, known for hopping quickly after ground balls, and Johnny "Crab" Evers. He crouched low to scoop up grounders. One of the team's stars in the 1970s was Ralph Garr. His quick bat and speedy legs earned him the nickname "Roadrunner." Greg Maddux pitched for the Braves until 2003. He often wore glasses and was dubbed "The Professor." Ronald Acuña's teammates began calling him "La Bestia" after he slugged a game winning homer in 2019, pounded his chest, and declared in Spanish "I am a beast!"

Braves

Third basemen Austin Riley

games. Still, the Braves continued their playoff streak. They were led by NL MVP Freddie Freeman, who batted .341, and lefty pitching ace Max Fried, who went 7–0 on the mound. The next year, they raced through the regular season and continued right through the playoffs to the 2021 World Series. Then, led by Freeman, slugging third baseman Austin Riley, and outfielder Jorge Soler, the Braves topped the Houston Astros to win the franchise's fourth world championship.

Atlanta continued to stay near the top of the NL standings in the 2020s. In both 2022 and 2023, the club won more than 100 games. The 104 wins in 2023 matched the all-time franchise high.

The Atlanta Braves are indeed a mixture of old and new. The Braves are the oldest franchise in Major League Baseball. Their history stretches back to 1871. Since that time, the franchise has thrilled fans in three home cities and across the nation. Loaded with young stars, the team now plays in an exciting new stadium. The Braves are ready to continue making baseball history in the Southeast for many seasons to come.

Outfielder Michael Harris II

INDEX